Our World of Information

What's It About?

Information Around Us

Claire Throp

Heinemann Library,
Chicago, IL

www.heinemannraintree.com
Visit our website to find out
more information about
Heinemann-Raintree books.

To order:

☎ Phone 888-454-2279

💻 Visit www.heinemannraintree.com
to browse our catalog and order online.

Edited by Rebecca Rissman and Catherine Veitch
Designed by Richard Parker
Original illustrations © Capstone Global Library
Illustrated by Darren Lingard
Picture research by Ruth Blair
Production by Duncan Gilbert
Originated by Heinemann Library
Printed in China by South China Printing Company Ltd

14 13 12 11 10
10 9 8 7 6 5 4 3 2 1

Library of Congress Cataloging-in-Publication Data

Throp, Claire.
  What's it about? : information around us / Claire Throp.
    p. cm. -- (Our world of information)
  Includes bibliographical references and index.
  ISBN 978-1-4329-3374-6 -- ISBN 978-1-4329-3380-7 (pbk.)
1. Information resources--Juvenile literature. I. Title.
  ZA3070.T487 2009
  020--dc22
                        2009004408

Acknowledgments

We would like to thank the following for permission to
reproduce photographs: Alamy pp. **9** (© Jupiterimages/
BananaStock), **10** (© Image Farm Inc.), **20** (© Thierry Cariou);
© Capstone Publishers pp. **17, 19 & 18** (Karon Dubke); Corbis
pp. **5** (Jim Craigmyle), **7** (Mihai Barbu/Reuters), **12** (Roy
McMahon), **13** (Alan Schein Photography), **14** (David P. Hall),
24 (Michel Touraine/Pixland), **25** (Marc Serota/Reuters), **27**
(Rainer Holz/Zefa), **29** (PlainPicture); Getty Images p. **15**
(Gen Nishino); iStockphoto p. **21** (© Mark Goddard);
Photoshot p. **11** (Imagebroker.net), **22** (Bader-Butowski).

Cover photograph of a woman using a cell phone on a busy
street reproduced with permission of Corbis (Yang Liu).

Every effort has been made to contact copyright holders
of any material reproduced in this book. Any omissions
will be rectified in subsequent printings if notice is given to
the publisher.

All the Internet addresses (URLs) given in this book were valid
at the time of going to press. However, due to the dynamic
nature of the Internet, some addresses may have changed, or
sites may have changed or ceased to exist since publication.
While the author and publisher regret any inconvenience this
may cause readers, no responsibility for any such changes can
be accepted by either the author or the publisher.

Contents

Any words appearing in the text in bold, **like this**, are explained in the glossary.

Information Is Everywhere

You are surrounded by information.
Information tells you about things.
Information comes in many different forms.
It can be words, pictures, films, sounds, or
graphic organizers.

 Information can be found in books
and newspapers, on the Internet,
and by asking questions.

Information is everywhere. Information can be found on Internet pages or in a list of phone numbers. Information can be heard through the radio or by the school bell ringing for the start of the day.

 Information can be found on cell phones.

Why Is Information Presented in Different Ways?

Information is presented in different ways so that many people can understand it. Some information is easier to understand when it is written out. Other information is easier to understand when it is in a chart or graph.

Method	Speed (miles per hour)
Walking	3
Cycling	15
Driving car in town	25
Driving car on highway	up to 75

Graphic organizers, such as this table, are good for showing certain types of information.

The siren on a fire truck makes a loud noise so that people can hear it even if they are in a car listening to music. People who are **visually impaired** may not be able to see signs or **symbols**. When they cross a street, they may listen for cars or for a beeping noise made when it is safe to cross.

 Emergency vehicles use a siren and flashing lights so people can hear and see them coming.

How Do Different Types Of Information Affect Us?

Information can affect you in many ways. When a word has been made bold in printed information, this tells you that the word is important.

Warning: Keep this product in a refrigerator.

 Labels help you stay healthy by telling you when and how you should eat food **products**.

Some information can be enjoyed, such as when you listen to a story or watch a movie.

Some information tells us to do things right away. For example, if you hear a fire alarm you need to leave the building quickly.

Signs

Signs are a common source of information. The information can be shown through a sign's color or shape. People who speak different languages can all understand what colors and shapes mean.

Warning signs are often shown in triangles.

 Many countries use similar signs for bathrooms.

Pictures on signs are usually very simple so people can easily understand them. A picture of a woman is usually used to show the women's bathroom. A picture of a person in a wheelchair shows that there is access for people who are disabled.

Signs With Words

 This sign tells people that the shop is closed.

Signs with words can give information such as the name of a school or the opening times of a library. Other signs can have pictures and words, such as a billboard. A billboard is a big sign used to **advertise** a **product** such as a type of food.

The size of the words on a sign depends on how far away people are likely to see it. For example, a sign that needs to be seen from a distance needs to have very large letters so that people can read it.

 Billboards can be seen from a long distance.

At Home

Information can be found all around you, even at home. You may have a chart on the wall in your home for household chores. This is so everyone knows when it is their turn to clean the yard or help with the dishes.

 Using a chart for household chores means that you will never forget to do your share.

Calendars are useful for everyone in the family.

A calendar shows the days, weeks, and months in a year. Calendars are useful because they help you keep track of what you are supposed to be doing each day. This means you can make sure you never miss swimming or soccer practice.

Packaging

CAUTION: Use with adequate ventilation. In case of eye contact, flush immediately with water for at least 15 minutes.

CAUTION: Causes eye and skin irritation. Do not get into eyes, on skin, or on clothing.

⚠ DANGER

CONTENTS ARE FLAMMABLE: Keep spray away from heat, sparks, pilot lights, open flames, etc. Unplug electrical tools, motors, and other appliances before spraying or bringing the can near any source of electricity.

 Many **products** have warning labels that tell you how to use the product safely. Always ask an adult to handle these products.

A lot of information can be found on packaging. For example, if you want to find out what ingredients are in your favorite food, you can look at the packaging. Food labels give information about the food, including how to cook and store it.

Safety information might be shown on the box holding a new toy. It might be shown in bold letters, **like this**, so that it stands out as being important.

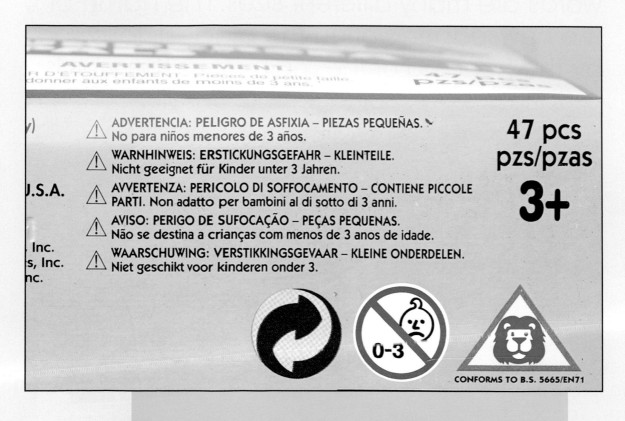

The information on a toy box might tell you for which age group the toy is made.

Electronic Information

There are many different types of electronic information. The Internet connects millions of computers, meaning a lot of information can be shared. **Online encyclopedias** and dictionaries allow you to search for information about a wide range of subjects.

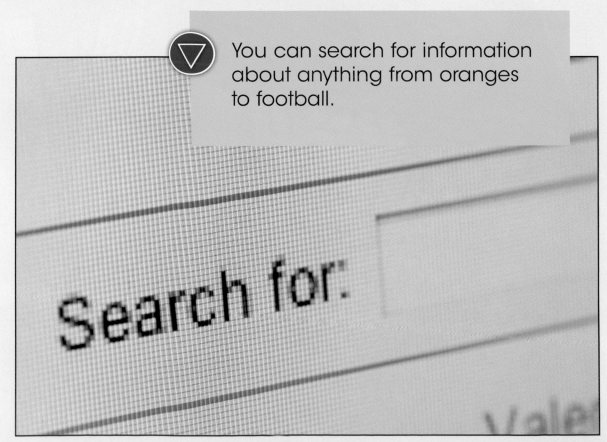

You can search for information about anything from oranges to football.

Ask if you need help finding information.

You can also use **multimedia discs** to find information. Some other types of electronic or online information are text messages, blogs, **wikis**, social Websites, and video or music Websites. New types of electronic and online information are always being made.

Television and Video

Television programs and videos can give information about many subjects. Television and videos can also be found on the Internet. You can either watch live **streaming** of the videos or **download** videos to watch later.

Watching television can be fun, and it can help you to learn new things, too.

Between and during television shows,
there are often a number of **commercials**.
Commercials try to sell things to the
people watching. They give a different
type of information from that shown on
television programs.

Sounds

Sounds can tell you information. An alarm clock rings so that you know it is time to get up in the morning. The theme music from your favorite television program tells you that it is about to begin.

 Hearing the school bell tells you that it is playtime.

You can often hear emergency vehicles before you can see them.

Sounds can also be warnings. For example, a siren warns drivers to get out of the way of a fire truck or an ambulance.

Information in Our Lives

Information is everywhere and is usually helpful to us. However, there is so much information in our world that it can sometimes be hard to know where to look or what to do.

 It is important to learn which information is worth paying attention to and which is not.

Information is presented in different ways so that you can understand it. Information can help you make decisions and understand your world. Information can help you learn new things.

 Finding out new information can be fun.

Activities

Different Information

Try spending a day looking for different types of information. Before you go out, draw a simple table, such as the one below, in a notebook. Take your notebook and a pen with you. Write down how many times you find each type of information.

Words	Pictures	Words and pictures	Film	Sound

Get together with a friend, and try "reading" pictures.

Reading Pictures

Look through a picture book with a friend and choose a picture. Each of you should try to write down three pieces of information from the picture. When you have finished, compare what you have written. Did you find the same information?

Glossary

advertise to tell people about something, often a product to be sold

commercial short program on television made by companies to get people to buy the DVDs, toys, or other things they make. Information in commercials is usually one-sided.

download moving information from the Internet to a personal computer or other electronic equipment. For example, you can download a music track from a Website to your computer. Before you download anything, ask an adult. Not all downloads are allowed or safe.

encyclopedia book with information about many subjects, or with a lot of information about a particular subject

graphic organizer way of showing information in a chart, table, or graph

multimedia disc disc that gives information in different forms such as sound, words, and video

online connected to the Internet

product something made by people, usually for selling. Toys or food are examples of products.

streaming when you can view information on the Internet right away without having to download it

symbol word or picture that stands for something else. For example, a triangle made up of three arrows is the sign for recycling.

visually impaired unable to see very well or at all

wiki Website that allows many people to add or change information

Find Out More

Doudna, Kelly. *I'll Use Information for My Explanation!* Edina, Minn.: ABDO Publishing, 2007.

Oxlade, Chris. *My First Internet Guide*. Chicago, Ill.: Heinemann Library, 2007.

Websites

Homework Help – Yahoo! Kids
http://kids.yahoo.com/learn
This web page includes links to an encyclopedia, dictionary, maps, and a lot of other useful Websites.

CBBC – Stay Safe
www.bbc.co.uk/cbbc/help/safesurfing
This Website gives you advice on staying safe while you are on the Internet.

Index